W9-ABU-037

EARTH CYCLES

ANIMAL LIFE CYCLES

by Sally Morgan

A+

Smart Apple Media

Published by Smart Apple Media
P.O. Box 3263, Mankato, Minnesota 56002

Printed in the United States of America at Corporate Graphics, in North Mankato, Minnesota.

Published by arrangement with the Watts Publishing Group Ltd., London.

Library of Congress Cataloging-in-Publication Data
Morgan, Sally, 1957-.
  Animal Life Cycles / by Sally Morgan.
     p. cm. -- (Earth cycles)
  Includes bibliographical references and index.
  Summary: "Describes the life cycles of different types of animals. Discusses how mature animals court, reproduce, and birth and care for their young and how young animals grow up and survive. Includes life cycle diagrams"--Provided by publisher.
  ISBN 978-1-59920-521-2 (library binding : alk. paper)
  1. Animal life cycles--Juvenile literature. I. Title.
  QL49.M7964 2012
  591.56--dc22

                              2010030424

Produced for Franklin Watts by
White-Thomson Publishing, Ltd.
Editor: Jean Coppendale
Design: Paul Manning

Picture credits
t = top b = bottom l = left = r = right
1, ECO/Mike Whittle; 3b, 12, Shutterstock/Carrydream; 3r, 9l, Shutterstock/EcoPrint; 4, ECO/Robert Pickett; 5l, Shutterstock/Sergey Kartashov; 5r, Shutterstock/Guentermanaus; 5b, Shutterstock/Christian Musat; 6t, ECO/Reinhard Dirscherl; 6b, 31, Shutterstock/Michelle D. Milliman; 7t, Shutterstock/FloridaStock; 7b, Shutterstock/Eric Gevaert; 7r, ECO/Robert Pickett; 8l, Shutterstock/Peter Betts; 8r, ECO/Fritz Polking; 9b, ECO/Fritz Polking; 9r, ECO/Reinhard Dirscherl; 10t, Shutterstock/Peter Ingvorsen; 11l, ECO/Robert Pickett; 11r, ECO/Michael Gore; 13t, ECO/John Lewis; 13b, ECO/Neil Miller; 13r, ECO/ Wayne Lawler; 14, ECO/Anthony Cooper; 15l, ECO/Robert Pickett; 15r, Shutterstock/Paul Cowan; 16, ECO/Robert Pickett; 17l, ECO/Robin Redfern; 17r, ECO/John Lewis; 18b, Shutterstock/Angela Hampton; 18t, ECO/Fritz Polking; 19l, Shutterstock/Mark R. Higgins; 19r, ECO/Frank Blackburn; 20t, ECO/Fritz Polking; 20b, Shutterstock/Cathy Keifer; 21l, ECO/Reinhard Dirscherl; 21r, Shutterstock/Malost; 22l, Shutterstock/SF Photo; 22c, ECO/Robert Pickett; 22r, Shutterstock/Jacob Hamblin; 23l, Shutterstock/Kurt G; 23c, Shutterstock/Cathy Keifer; 23b, ECO/Robert Pickett; 23r, ECO/Robert Pickett; 24t, ECO/John Liddiard; 24b, Shutterstock/Anke van Wyk; 25l, ECO/Robert Pickett; 25r, ECO/John Lewis; 26b, Shutterstock/Judex; 27r, Shutterstock/Nick Stubbs; 28l, Shutterstock/Caroline Tolsma; 29l, Shutterstock/Dave Allen Photography; 29r, Shutterstock/Ingvars Birznieks; 29b, Shutterstock/Javarman; 30, Shutterstock/Nagy Melinda. Cover images: ECO/Mike Whittle (main); Shutterstock/Paul Cowman (egg); ECO/Fritz Polking.

Note to parents and teachers
Every effort has been made by the publishers to ensure that the web sites listed on page 32 are suitable for children, that they are of the highest educational value, and that they contain no inappropriate or offensive material. However, because of the nature of the Internet, it is impossible to guarantee that the contents of these sites have not been altered. We strongly advise that Internet access is supervised by a responsible adult.

1466

3-2012

9 8 7 6 5 4

Contents

Words appearing in **bold** like this can be found in the Glossary on pages 30-31.

What Is an Animal?

All animals have some **features** in common. For example, they can **reproduce**, and they need food to eat so that they can grow. Unlike plants that make their own food, animals have to find their food in order to survive.

Backbones

Animals can be divided into two groups—**vertebrates** and **invertebrates**. Vertebrates are animals with backbones. A backbone is a flexible rod of small bones that runs down the back of animals such as birds, fish, and **mammals**. Invertebrates are animals that do not have a backbone. They include insects, **mollusks**, **sea anemones**, and worms.

▼ The giant panda is a type of mammal that lives in China. It spends at least 12 hours a day eating bamboo.

▼ **Reptiles,** such as this iguana, are vertebrates.

Q Which animal spends its life upside down?

A The sloth. The sloth is a mammal that lives in the Amazon rain forest in South America. It hangs from branches using its long claws. It eats, sleeps, and even gives birth upside down.

▲ Sloth

Life Cycles

Young animals grow and change into adults. Some changes are gradual. A newborn puppy looks like a small adult dog, and it gradually gets larger. Other animals go through big changes in appearance. For example, a butterfly **egg** hatches into a **larva,** called a caterpillar. It looks more like a worm than an adult butterfly. The body of the caterpillar has to change to become the adult. This change is called **metamorphosis.**

▼ The caterpillar of the swallowtail butterfly

All Types of Animals

Animals range in size from tiny animals such as the **amoeba**, which is only 0.03 inch (1 mm) across, to the blue whale, the world's largest animal, which can grow up to 100 feet (30 m) long.

▼ Whales are the largest animals. These humpback whales grow to about 50 feet (15 m) long, and their flippers are one-third of their body length.

Animal Species

Scientists have identified about 1.5 million **species** of animals. Each species is unique or different from all other species. But there are many millions of species still waiting to be discovered. These animals live in the unexplored habitats of the world, such as remote rain forests and deep oceans.

▶ This fire-bellied toad is one of 6,400 known species of **amphibians**.

Animal Features

An animal is identified by its features. For example, insects have six legs, while spiders have eight legs. Birds are covered in feathers, and fish are covered in scales. Some animals, such as birds and fish, lay eggs. Most mammals give birth to live young.

▲ A bird, such as this bald eagle, is covered with feathers, and it has wings instead of arms.

Q What is a fossil?

A A fossil is the preserved remains of an ancient animal or plant. Most fossils, such as the **ammonite** below, are found in rocks. They help scientists learn about animals that lived millions of years ago.

▲ Ammonite fossil

Grouping Animals

There are so many animals that scientists put them into groups according to their features. Vertebrates are divided into fish, amphibians, reptiles, birds, and mammals. Each of these groups is divided into smaller and smaller groups containing fewer species. For example, human beings belong to the **primate** group within mammals. Primates are divided into **lemurs**, monkeys, and apes. Humans are a type of ape.

▶ This macaque monkey is a type of primate.

Life of an Animal

An animal's life cycle involves birth, growing up, adulthood, and death.

Eggs or Live Young?

Life for all animals begins in an egg. The egg contains the **embryo**, which grows into a young animal. Some female animals lay eggs and these hatch into young. Insects, fish, and birds all lay eggs. Female mammals keep their eggs inside their body. The embryo grows, and after a certain period of time, the female gives birth to a baby animal.

Life of Mammals

The life cycle of a mammal starts with mating and the birth of live young. Young mammals rely on their mothers for milk. They grow and become adults.

1
▲ A male and female lion come together to mate.

2
▲ A female lion is called a lioness. She gives birth to up to four cubs and feeds the cubs with her milk.

Q and A

Q Which animal can change sex?

A Fish. Many fish found on coral reefs, such
as clown fish and wrasses, can change sex.
If a large male dies, a female becomes
a male to replace him. Scientists are
still unsure about how and why
this happens. It's one of the
mysteries of the reef.

3

▲ The cubs grow quickly.
Lions reach adulthood
at about 2–3 years of age
and are ready to mate.

▲ Clown fish

Mature Mammals

When the adults
are mature, they
are ready to
reproduce and
have young of their
own. The final stage
of the life cycle is the
death of the animal. Its
body rots and the **nutrients**
are usually returned to
the ground.

4

▲ Lions in the wild live
for about 12 years.

9

Courtship

The first stage in the life cycle of an animal is when the male and female animal pair off. Animals have many ways to attract a mate.

Choosing the Best

An animal may choose a mate by appearance. Some female birds may choose the male with the most colorful feathers. Others pick the male with the best song or the biggest nest. Many male mammals fight other males for females.

▲ Female peacocks choose the males with the longest tail feathers.

▼ These two male wildebeests are fighting over a female. They face each other on their knees and push against each other with their thick horns.

Q and A

Time of Year

Some females can only mate at certain times of the year. This may be to ensure that the young are born at a time of the year when there is food. Often, the male knows when the time is right by the female's smell or appearance. For example, female butterflies and moths release a smelly substance that the males can detect with their long **antennae**.

Q Which male bird collects gifts to impress a mate?

A The bowerbird. The male builds a bower, or nest, to impress the female. It is built from twigs, which the male sticks in the ground. The male bowerbird decorates his bower with objects that he finds in the forest and calls to the female to come and look.

female ⎯⎯ male

▲ Bowerbirds

Courting

Some animals carry out a pattern of behavior called **courtship**, such as a dance or giving gifts. The bird of paradise and the red-crowned crane carry out complex courtship dances. Some male fish **display** to the female. The male stickleback builds a nest and displays in front of it to attract a mate.

◀ Male and female red-crowned cranes pair for life. The pair perform a courtship dance of bows, head-bobbing, and leaps.

Reproduction

Reproduction in most animals involves two parents—a male and a female. This is called sexual reproduction.

▼ The male and female butterfly mate. The male butterfly places sperm inside the female to fertilize the eggs.

When animals are ready to reproduce, they produce **gametes**. These are special sex cells. The gametes produced by the male are called spermatozoa, or sperm for short. The female produces gametes called eggs. When a male and a female animal mate, the sperm is transferred to the female.

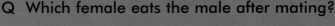

Fertilization

The next stage is **fertilization**, when a single sperm joins with an egg to produce an embryo. The embryo grows into a new individual. With animals such as fish, fertilization takes place outside the body of the male and female as the eggs and sperm are released into the water. In animals such as mammals and birds, fertilization takes place inside the female. Then the female either lays an egg or gives birth to live young.

▼ These anglerfish eggs are 4–5 weeks old and have well-developed embryos.

Q Which female eats the male after mating?

A The black widow spider. This spider gets its name because occasionally the female spider eats the male after mating. This happens with other spiders, too, especially the Australian red-back spider. Sometimes the male is eaten because the female mistakes him for **prey**!

Asexual Reproduction

In a few animals, reproduction occurs without two parents. This is called **asexual reproduction**. All offspring (young) produced asexually are identical to each other and to the parent animal. For example, the amoeba is a tiny **single-celled** animal found in water that reproduces asexually. It simply divides into two, and each part grows into a new animal.

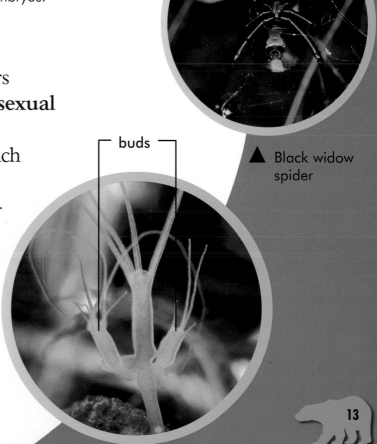

buds

▲ Black widow spider

► The hydra is a small animal that reproduces asexually. This hydra has two buds, which are miniature hydra. They are about to break off.

13

Laying Eggs

Most animals lay eggs, except for mammals. A fertilized egg contains an embryo and a store of food, called the yolk. The eggs of fish and amphibians have a protective jelly coating. Reptiles lay eggs with a leathery shell, and birds lay eggs with hard shells. Insects, such as butterflies, also lay eggs with a shell.

Many or Few?

Most fish lay thousands and sometimes millions of eggs. This is because most of the eggs are eaten by other animals. Only a few young fish hatch and grow to adulthood. This means the fish lays many eggs to make sure that some survive. Animals, such as birds and reptiles, lay fewer, but larger eggs. These eggs are usually protected or hidden, so most of them survive and hatch.

▲ The frog lays its eggs in water. Each egg has a protective jelly coating.

Scattered Eggs

Animals that live in water, such as fish, usually scatter their eggs in the water. Some animals bury their eggs in the ground like turtles and crocodiles do. Most birds lay their eggs in nests where the female bird **incubates** them (keeps them warm) until they are ready to hatch. Butterflies lay their eggs on plants, either singly or in groups.

Q Which bird lays the largest egg?

A The ostrich. The egg of the ostrich weighs up to 4.5 pounds (2 kg) and is about the weight and size of more than 20 chicken eggs. An ostrich egg takes an hour to boil!

ostrich egg

chicken egg

▲ The garden snail lays clusters of about 70 to 90 round white eggs and buries them in the soil.

New Life

After a certain length of time, the egg hatches or the female gives birth to her young. The period of time between fertilization and birth is called the **gestation** period. This can be as short a time as a few weeks in kangaroos, but as long as two years for an elephant.

Hatching

When a chick is ready to hatch, it uses a small tooth on top of its beak to break through the shell and push itself out. It does not need to feed for the first day as it uses up the food stored within its body. Some chicks have fluffy feathers and can run within minutes, but others are born without feathers and are helpless.

▼ This chick has just hatched. It is able to stand up and follow its mother.

Giving Birth

When the time comes to give birth, female mammals usually move to a safe, sheltered place to have their young. Many give birth at dawn or dusk when there are fewer **predators** around. They may build a nest to keep their young warm.

Q Which male gives birth to young?

A The sea horse. The male and female do a courtship dance when they wrap their tails around each other. The female lays her eggs in a pouch on the male's **abdomen** where they are fertilized. He keeps the eggs in his pouch for up to four weeks and then the tiny sea horses hatch.

▲ Baby mice are born with no fur, their eyes are closed, and they cannot hear. They stay in the nest and feed on their mother's milk.

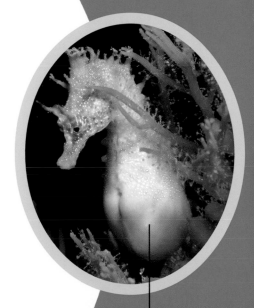

The eggs are in the male seahorse's pouch.

Litter Sizes

Large mammals, such as humans, gorillas, and whales, usually give birth to only one baby. Smaller mammals, such as cats, dogs, and rats, give birth to a litter of several babies. Some of the largest litters are born to mice and **opossums**. Tenrecs are small mole-like mammals, and they may have as many as 30 babies at one time.

Caring for Young

Many egg-laying animals simply lay their eggs and leave them, but other animals care for their babies.

Giving Milk

All female mammals produce milk to feed their young. Milk is a liquid food that contains all the nutrients needed by the growing mammal. Some newborn mammals feed on milk for just a few days before they start eating solid food. Others feed for much longer. A young elephant, for example, feeds on its mother's milk for up to two years.

▲ These emperor penguin checks have been left together in a **crèche** while their parents hunt for fish.

▼ A newborn lamb stands up within minutes of being born. It is licked dry by its mother, and then it **suckles** her milk.

Feeding Young

Growing animals have huge appetites. A robin chick, for example, needs to eat every hour. This means that parent birds spend hours each day finding food for their hungry chicks. Predators, such as lionesses and tigers, hunt for deer and other animals to feed their cubs.

Q Which bird lays its eggs in another bird's nest?

A The cuckoo. The female cuckoo lays an egg that is similar in color to the other eggs in the nest. The cuckoo chick hatches first and grows faster and larger than the other chicks. Usually it pushes all the other chicks out of the nest, so it is the only chick and gets all the food.

Guarding Babies

Most parents guard their offspring from predators. For example, a herd of musk oxen forms a circle around their calves if wolves come near. Rhinos and elephants attack any animal that threatens their young. Some parent animals will run or fly away, hoping to draw the predator away from where they have left their babies.

cuckoo chick

parent dunnock bird

◀ Kangaroos carry their young, called joeys, around in their pouch where they are protected.

19

Growing Up

The next stage in the life of the animal is growing up. Over time, the animal grows larger and becomes an adult animal ready to **breed**.

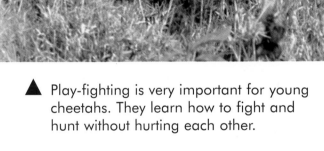

Learning to Hunt

Young predators have to learn how to hunt. If they do not have these skills, they will die of hunger. Many mammals, such as cheetahs and lions, learn from their mothers. They go with her when she hunts, and when they are large enough, they join in.

▲ Play-fighting is very important for young cheetahs. They learn how to fight and hunt without hurting each other.

Getting Larger

Reptiles, insects, and crabs have a tough **skeleton** around the outside of their body. This causes problems when they grow because the skeleton does not stretch. This is a bit like wearing clothes that are too small. To grow larger, they must shed their skeleton and grow a new, larger one. This is called **molting**.

molting skin

▲ Chameleons have to molt to grow because their scaly skin cannot expand.

Life in the Ocean

Many young fish spend the first months of their lives as **plankton**, floating in the upper layer of the water. Here, they feed and grow. The salmon is unusual because the young salmon hatch in freshwater but grow to adulthood in saltwater. They return to freshwater to breed. The turtle lays its eggs in the sand on beaches. A couple of months later, the hatchlings emerge. They have to dash to the sea to escape the many birds, crabs, and other predators waiting on the beach.

Q Which baby can triple its weight in three weeks?

A An elephant seal pup. The mother's milk is rich in fat, so the pup grows quickly for three or four weeks, and a thick layer of **blubber** forms under the skin. When its mother leaves, the young pup has to look after itself. It survives on its blubber while it learns how to catch food.

▲ Elephant seal pup

▲ Young turtles stay at sea for many years, slowly getting larger. Then they return to the beaches where they were born to breed.

21

Metamorphosis

Metamorphosis means to change in shape. This change is an important part of the life cycle of animals such as amphibians and insects.

The Butterfly's Life Cycle

A butterfly is a type of insect. It has four stages in its life cycle. The adult butterfly lays eggs, which hatch into caterpillars. The caterpillar is the growing stage of the life cycle. Caterpillars feed and grow, and when they reach full size, they molt for the last time and become a **pupa**. Inside the pupa, the body of the caterpillar is rearranged into the body of an adult. When the change is complete, the pupa splits open and a new adult butterfly emerges.

◄ The adult butterfly feeds on flowers and lays its eggs on a leaf.

1

egg

2

caterpillar

3

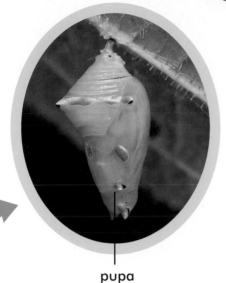

pupa

Q Which tadpole never grows up?

A The axolotl. The axolotl is a type of amphibian. Unlike other amphibians, the tadpole of the axolotl never changes shape when it becomes an adult but stays as a large tadpole with gills for its entire life. It never undergoes metamorphosis.

4

▶ The case of the pupa splits open and an adult butterfly emerges.

Amphibians

Amphibians are animals that live part of their lives in water and part on land. Frogs are amphibians. The female frog lays her eggs in water where they are fertilized. After a week or so, the larvae, called tadpoles, hatch. The tadpoles look a bit like small fish. Over the next couple of months, the tadpoles gradually change in appearance, becoming more like a frog. They grow four legs, their body shape changes, and their tail shrinks. Then they are ready to leave the water.

▲ Axolotl

▼ This tadpole has grown four legs and now its tail will shrink.

Finding Food

Animals cannot make their own food as plants do, so they have to find a ready-made source of food, such as other animals. All the animals and plants living in the same place are **dependent** on each other. They form a **food chain**.

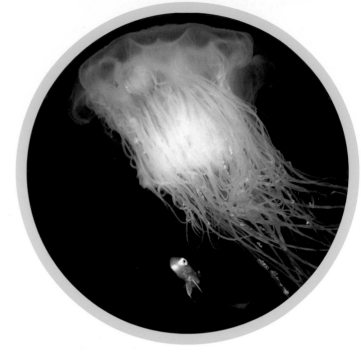

Eating Plants

Many animals feed on plants, especially the leaves, fruit, and roots. These animals are known as herbivores. Meat-eating animals are called carnivores. Carnivores are predators because they feed on other animals.

▲ Jellyfish feed on small fish and plankton. In turn, they are eaten by turtles, crabs, and some fish.

▼ The giraffe is a herbivore. It uses its long tongue to pull leaves off trees.

Catching Prey

Predators are usually larger
and fewer in number than their
prey. Each has a different way of
catching its prey. For example, spiders spin
a web of sticky threads to catch flying insects.

Q Which fish fishes for food?

A The anglerfish. It has a long spine that sticks
out from the middle of its head with a knob
at the end. It dangles this to attract
small fish, and when they get
close, the anglerfish grabs
them in its wide mouth.

horseshoe-
shaped knob
on long spine

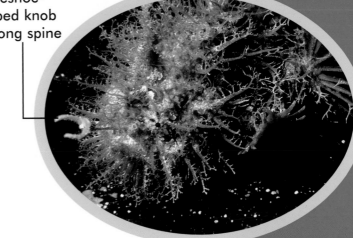

◀ The lynx feeds on
smaller animals
such as pheasants
and rabbits.

▲ The tassled
anglerfish
tricks small
fish with its
seaweed-like
camouflage
and attracts
them with its
horseshoe-
shaped "bait"
on the end of
its long spine.

Waiting for Food

Some predators wait for their prey to come close and
then jump out on them. They rely on **camouflage** so
that they are not noticed. For example, frogfish have
an irregular shape to blend in with the rocks and coral
on which they rest. Crab spiders are the same color
as the flower in which they hide. Flat fish, such as
turbot, lie just under the surface of the seabed so
they cannot be spotted.

Scavengers

When animals die, their bodies become food for other animals called **scavengers**. Without scavengers, the bodies of dead animals would pile up everywhere.

▼ A vulture has excellent eyesight. This means it can spot dead bodies on the ground from far away.

Vultures

Vultures are common scavengers in many countries, where they are seen circling high in the sky. A group of vultures quickly removes all the edible parts of a body, leaving just bits of skin and bone. Some vultures have featherless necks so they can place their head inside a dead body without covering their feathers in blood and rotting meat.

Small Scavengers

Amongst the smaller scavengers are beetles and maggots. Many types of flies lay their eggs on dead bodies so their larvae, called maggots, have plenty of food. Within a few days, all the soft parts of the dead body are gone.

◄ Maggots feed on dead remains and then **pupate**. Adult flies hatch a few days later.

Q and A

▼ Hyenas and jackals scavenge for food on the African **savanna**.

Q Which animal's favorite food is dung?

A The **dung** beetle. Dung beetles' excellent sense of smell allows them to detect dung as soon as it hits the ground, and then there is a race to get to it first. The beetles break off small pieces and roll them along before burying them. Dung is so precious that dung beetles steal the dung balls from other beetles.

▲ Dung beetles

Bacteria and Fungi

These tiny **decomposers** feed on animal dung as well as dead bodies. They release chemicals called enzymes that break down the remains and make them into a liquid. The decomposers absorb, or take in, this liquid. During this process, some of the nutrients from the remains are released into the ground where they are taken in by plant roots. The cycle then begins again.

How Long Do Animals Live?

Some animals live for just a day or so, but others can live for hundreds of years.

Record Breakers

One of the longest-living animals is the giant tortoise, a type of reptile. Giant tortoises are found on islands such as the Galapagos and Seychelles. Several giant tortoises are known to have lived for 175 years or more. Other animals with long lives include humans and elephants at 70 years, crocodiles at 50 to 70 years, and swans that live to more than 100 years of age.

▼ Giant tortoises grow very slowly all through their long lives. They can weigh up to 660 pounds (300 kg).

Long Cycle

Insects can also live long lives. The cicada, a type of bug, spends up to 17 years as a larva in the ground. Then the adult emerges, breeds, and dies within a few weeks.

◀ A cicada has the longest-known life span of any insect.

Q What is the world's oldest animal?

A A clam living in waters off the coast of Norway. This particular clam may be 400 years old. On land, a giant tortoise named Tu'i Malila was believed to have lived to 188 years.

▲ Clam

Heartbeats

Usually a smaller mammal has a shorter life than a large mammal. Some scientists think this is due to the number of times its heart beats. They estimate that a mammal's heart can beat about one billion times. Mice have hearts that beat very fast, so they use up their billion beats in just four years. Elephants have a slow-beating heart and therefore live longer.

▶ Elephants can live for over 70 years.

Glossary

abdomen the part of the body between an animal's chest and hips

ammonite a mollusk with a coiled shell that lived in the oceans hundreds of millions of years ago

amoeba a single-celled animal that lives in water

amphibian an animal such as a frog or toad that lives in water and on land

antenna a feeler, used by insects such as butterflies to detect smell

asexual reproduction a form of reproduction where an individual makes a copy of itself by budding or dividing without the involvement of another individual

blubber a layer of fat beneath the skin that helps keep an animal warm

breed to reproduce

camouflage coloring that blends with the background

courtship behavior such as dancing that some animals perform before mating

crèche a group of young animals left together; older penguin chicks are left in a crèche while their parents feed.

decomposer an organism that breaks down dead and decaying matter

dependent reliant on another

display to show or perform

dung animal droppings

egg the first stage in the life cycle of an animal; the embryo develops within the egg.

embryo the first stage of a new life produced when an egg and sperm join together

feature a characteristic, a part of the appearance of an animal

fertilization the joining together of an egg and sperm

food chain feeding relationships between plants, herbivores, and carnivores

gamete the special sex cells made by animals for reproduction

gestation the period of time between fertilization and birth

incubate to keep eggs warm while the embryo develops inside

invertebrate an animal without a backbone

larva the growing stage of an animal such as an insect

lemur a type of primate found in Madagascar, an island off the east coast of southern Africa

mammal a vertebrate animal that is covered with hair; the female gives birth to live young and feeds them with her own milk.

metamorphosis a change in the appearance of an animal in its life cycle

mollusk an invertebrate with a muscular foot and a shell outside or inside its body; snails, octopus, and squid are mollusks.

molt when an animal sheds or gets rid of old skin, hair, feathers, or outer skeletons to grow larger

nutrient a substance found in food or in the soil that is needed for organisms to grow

opossum a mammal that carries its young in a pouch, found in North, South, and Central America

plankton tiny plants and animals that float in the upper layer of seas and oceans

predator an animal that hunts other animals for food

prey animals that are eaten by predators

primate a type of mammal; monkeys and apes are primates.

pupa in insects, the stage in the life cycle between larva and adult

pupate when a larva turns into a pupa

reproduce to produce offspring

reptile a vertebrate with scaly skin

savanna vast plains of grass in Africa

scavenger an animal that feeds on the dead remains of other animals

sea anemone a marine invertebrate with tentacles that are covered in stinging cells

single-celled consisting of just one cell, the building block from which all organisms are composed

skeleton the part of the body that gives support and protection; it may be inside or around the outside of an animal's body.

species a group of organisms with the same features that can breed with each other

suckle to suck or drink milk from the mother

vertebrate an animal with a backbone

Further Reading

Guillain, Charlotte. *Life Cycles.* Heinemann Library, 2008.

Head, Honor. *Amazing Mammals.* Gareth Stevens Pub., 2008.

Weber, Belinda. *I Wonder Why Caterpillars Eat So Much and Other Questions About Life Cycles.* Kingfisher, 2006.

Web Sites

All About Frogs for Kids and Teachers: www.kiddyhouse.com/Themes/frogs
Information about the life cycle of a frog

Life of a Butterfly—Butterfly and Moth Life Cycle: www.lifeofabutterfly.com/lifecycle.html
Information about the stages of butterfly and moth lives

Mammals, Mammal Pictures, Facts About Mammals—National Geographic:
http://animals.nationalgeographic.com/animals/mammals/
Learn all you wanted to know about mammals with pictures, videos, photos, facts, and news from National Geographic.

Index